BOYS
VS
MEN

THE DEFINITION OF A MAN

Man/noun
Societal
1. A male over the age of 18 years old
   living in a constant state of self destruction.

Noah N. Johnson

Boys VS Men: The Definition of a Man

Noah N. Johnson

Published by

It's All 1 Luv

To contact, or to book Noah Johnson for an event, visit:

BoysVSMen.com

ISBN-13: 978-0692876732 (It's All 1 Luv)

ISBN-10: 0692876731

To all young men who lost their lives in an

attempt to become other people's

definition of a **_MAN_**.

Foreword

Boys vs. Men is a breath of fresh air for young men who have realized society's expectations for them may not match well with the man they would like to be. In a world where young men receive mixed messages from a very young age as to what a man should be, this is a wonderful guide to help them seek clarity as to the kind of man they would like to become. This book is unique in that it does not assume to have all the answers. Rather, it calls upon the reader to turn inward, to think and feel the material, honoring the individual and the dialectical nature of true growth. The flow and contents lend themselves to various settings as well; this text would work well for a person to use individually, or practitioners wishing to facilitate growth in one-on-one or group settings. Like sharp shears for a gardener and his tree, Boys vs. Men is a valuable tool, helping him to prune away material that is hindering growth. Just as pruning a tree will help it reach and grow to its full potential, so will using this book to prune away unwanted concepts about being a man in today's society. The reader will be compelled to develop their own definition of manhood, while embarking on the priceless journey of searching for one's soul.

-Elizabeth McGregor, MS, LMFT.

Introduction

I could be enrolled in school for the rest of my life, obtain every degree imaginable, and still not be better equipped than I am right now to define what it is to be a **MAN**. Because nobody can define it but you. There's no cookie cutter definition that fits us all, or that we would all want to fit. But I'm sure we all have an idea of what we believe or have been taught a man should be. I can't agree with the traditional definition that you'll find in a dictionary, because I know adult males that don't carry themselves as I think a man should. I have also known men that were 15 or 16 years old. I'm at the point of writing all of this because I strongly disagree with what society says a man should be (the definition on the front cover).

I started this book with the word "I" for a reason. This is written through experiences I have had throughout my journey from boy to man. Everyone's journey is different and I am presenting facts from my own life, completely expecting to be disagreed with on at least some of my perspectives. I look forward to being wrong. I am not writing this in an attempt to have anyone agree with me. Whether you agree or disagree isn't the point, the point is for you to become more confident that whatever you believe is a decision you made yourself, and not just something you were told to believe as a boy.

We are taught so much as kids and a lot of the teachings get carried into adulthood unquestioned. We are not allowed to talk to other boys or men about things because part of the definition most of us live by tells us we can't, so we inherently don't. How can we find our own truth if we haven't explored the truth of others? Our perspectives are just that, they are our own, but only a small piece of reality. I learned a lot about myself writing this and became more sure of myself and the kind of man I wanted to be. The hope is that the same exploration carries similar results for those reading it. Your age doesn't matter, any age is the right age to explore your beliefs.

Bio.

My mother is the strongest, smartest, most resilient, selfless, hard-working person I have ever known. Period. I owe her more than I probably even realize, and I realize I owe her a lot. She raised four kids while working two to three jobs sometimes and putting herself through school to earn multiple degrees. She always put her kids first and sacrificed everything to be in a position to constantly evolve and provide better for us. She instilled a lot of morals in us and was/is still a great teacher. She did her best in everything she did and even when things went wrong I know she always did what she felt was right. She was both my mother and father. I even get her a Father's Day card to say thanks for being that role in my life as well... But that's the importance of me writing all that about her, nobody could have done more than she did, but she couldn't show me how to be a **MAN**.

I never felt an emptiness not having my father in my life, but looking back at my actions I can see how much I needed and searched for guidance. I have a brother two years older than me, but him being in the same situation, he didn't have the answers either. Growing up I was the sick kid, always in and out of the hospital with my asthma. My mother was protective of us and I had a short leash when I was young, but when I was around 11 that changed. I wanted independence. My brother went on to high school and was finding his way, so I started to try to find my way as a man. I think not having any control over situations in my life made me take it to the extreme and try to control everything. Got me in a lot of trouble. Mostly petty stuff until I got older. When I was 15, my brother moved with my uncle seven hours away and by 16 I was fighting, selling drugs, and ready to prove I was a man in any way possible. By 17 I was a grown man and nobody could tell me different, I had it all figured out and I knew how life worked. I got close to an older guy who was showing me how to survive and he became that father figure I never had. We would go to hell and back together, it wasn't a positive relationship but we always had each other's back and it was nice to belong to something and be respected for being a man. We were close and he was the only male influence I personally had, so when he got killed I was thrown. Life pretty much stopped for a while.

I think not knowing you're lost is the worst part because you'll never ask for directions or pull your phone out to navigate if you think you know where you're going. I only knew one way to act as a man, so I continued the same attitude and kept getting into trouble and being the **_MAN_** I knew I was. When I was 18 I thought I was going to get into some serious trouble for my violence, so I enrolled myself in anger management. I wasn't really ready to change because I didn't fully understand I needed to. I was being exactly what I thought a man was, so why change? Some of what my anger management counselor was saying started to make sense. I even brought my boy with me to hear what he was saying sometimes. No matter how much sense he made though, we weren't changing the way we were living, or carrying ourselves as men. My boy got into a fight and I didn't think much of it, he was 16 and doing his thing. I never imagined they would throw gang enhancements on him and give him 12 years in prison. 12 years. My eyes were open.

After everything I had done and been through, that was the single biggest event that changed my life. I felt like a truck hit me. I had lost my influence a couple years before, and now my boy, who I should have been a better influence on gets 12 years in prison.

I cut everyone off and stopped hanging out. I spent the next few years finding myself, studying, writing, searching. Lost.

I lived more than 3 years suicidal feeling like everything was a lie, questioning reality, myself and my beliefs. It didn't make sense why I was still here but I lost so many other people and I had done things much worse. Every day for those 3 years I couldn't manage much else but trying to defend myself from my thoughts. I had no purpose and the only thing that saved me was finding one using my experiences to prevent others from having the same.

I hooked back up with my anger management counselor and his

cousin to talk about their plans. Together we spent the next few years starting an African American family and cultural center in my hometown. The first thing we did, even before we had any funding or a building, was start a book club with younger men to read and discuss books that related to our own lives. Having the books available to read was huge, but the biggest and most important piece to it was the group. Reading passages in the book together and stopping to have respectful conversations where everyone could express their own views and learn from one another was monumental. I never forgot that and took that general idea of open-minded idea sharing with me throughout all my work and life experiences.

Moving on from that, I spent the next seven years working with youth and using my life experiences to educate and relate to them. I've worked at youth centers, juvenile detention centers, group homes, schools, military institutions, and churches. I have built and facilitated hundreds of programs and the biggest progress I have ever seen in people has been through programs built in a way that allows open-minded conversations. Now I'm here, at a point in my life where everything seems to have intentionally brought me to.

Inspiration

"If there's a book that you want to read, but it hasn't been written yet, then you must write it."

- Toni Morrison

I never imagined writing a book, but after spending many years working with youth, especially young men, I saw a need that was unmet. Through these experiences I was constantly reminded of my own upbringing, trying to become a man without having an accurate example of what it was to be a man. My influences were Hip Hop music and guys following the same examples. With Hip Hop guiding our culture, and the direction of it seemingly going toward emasculated self-defeat, there needs to be conversation now more than ever. I grew up with both sides, a balance between street life and personal growth both being expressed with my three biggest influences being Tupac, Nas and DMX (if you don't know, artists like these expressed what was going on, the life they lived and also spoke on uplifting themselves and others past it). We are now mentally beaten into submission by our peers if we disagree with what we're told to think. Personal opinion isn't tolerated, and if we disagree with what we're told to like, or have our own thought, we are told something is wrong with us. If you don't like what the media tells you to like you are labeled a "HATER." I worked with a 7th-grade young man who told a group of "Popular kids" he didn't like a certain rapper, they all got on him calling him a hater like he isn't entitled to having an opinion that doesn't agree with what he was told to think. It's a tactic used by companies and media to keep people buying and believing what they are told to buy/believe by making you feel isolated if you don't. If you don't like something popular, everyone around you will look at you or treat you like something's wrong with you. It happens to me and I'm a grown man, I just grew up in a time where people were allowed to disagree with popular opinion. I can only imagine the pressure young men feel now when they are told they can't have an opinion of their own. Brilliant marketing strategy, but horrible lifestyle.

I am writing this because my experience tells me that young men and adults alike could benefit from examining their own thoughts and having an opportunity to be in a safe space for their personal thought to be explored. Whether as part of a group, sharing their opinions on the topics presented, or by yourself in your own head. If you live your entire life thinking things have to be how they are simply because that's the way they are, then your truth is only true due to a lack of alternatives. To me, being a man is standing by your thoughts and being sure in who you are and what you believe, which is

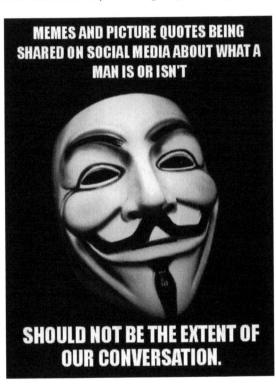

MEMES AND PICTURE QUOTES BEING SHARED ON SOCIAL MEDIA ABOUT WHAT A MAN IS OR ISN'T

SHOULD NOT BE THE EXTENT OF OUR CONVERSATION.

almost impossible if you haven't questioned the reasons you believe what you do. Nobody should be able to tell you what you believe, and if they have, can you truly believe it without first questioning it? My inspiration for this is not to change anyone's thought to mine, it is to present alternate truths that inspire thought and discussion, to either have you become more secure in your own beliefs, or to discover what it is that is true for you. To live your life as a man you created, and decided to be.

How this book works:

This book works pretty much however you want it to work for you. There are 52 chapters or subjects. That can be 52 weeks, 52 days, 52 hours, or minutes or whatever way works best for you. It's 100% ready to personalize for what works best for your group, or yourself. It's set up in a way where you can use this as a workbook as part of a weekly group of young men coming together and discuss personal opinions on the topics presented, or for you to go through it at a pace that works best for you. Each chapter is accompanied by a page with space that allows you to write out your opinions about the topic and/or writings in that chapter, questions you might want to ask other people in your group, why you agree or disagree with the passage or whatever you want to write there. This is a space for you. This book is not about me, it's not about your friends, it's not about your brother or father, it's not about what you're told to think, it's about you. It's about your freedom. Your thoughts, your opinions, your definition of a _**MAN**_.

Table of Contents

<u>Boys VS Men</u>
1- Adversity

Boys- Allows Life To Change Them.

Men- Are Constantly Evolving.

Life happens, boys change because of it, men adapt and evolve because of it. It's similar to the old saying, "What doesn't kill you only makes you stronger." I don't believe that's always the case, but similarly, boys break and men build. Adversity, and how you handle it is what defines your character. We will all experience our own adversity, boys allow it to change them, men allow it to be the catalyst for personal evolution. The question adversity often presents, and the choice you always have is, "Are you going to allow life to break you or build you?"

☐ Agree   ☐ Disagree   ☐ Both

BOYS

Why I feel this way

VS

MEN

_____

_____

_____

_____

_____

_____

THE DEFINITION OF A MAN

_____

_____

My definition of _____

_____

_____

<u>Boys VS Men</u>
2- Responsibility

Boys- Believe Men Do What They Want.

Men- Believe Men Do What Needs To Be Done.

The older I get, the more real this is to me. So many young men grow up not wanting to be told what to do. Can't get "punked", can't let someone control you. But the reality is, when I had that mentality when I was younger trying to be grown, I never got forced to do things more in my life! I was getting controlled by my environment, my friends, older guys, and the game I was playing. Men do what they have to do. Period. They don't have to like it, they just have to know it's what needs to be done. You think people like getting up every morning for work? You think they like having bills? Letting their boss talk to them the way they do? The answer is an emphatic NO! Men do what needs to be done to get the result they want. Nobody on this planet gets to do what they want without suffering the consequences. The more you do what needs to be done though, the more control over your life you take back.

BOYS

VS

MEN

☐   ☐   ☐
Agree   Disagree   Both

Why I feel this way

_____

_____

_____

_____

_____

_____

_____

THE DEFINITION OF A MAN

_____

_____

My definition of _____

_____

_____

Boys VS Men
3- Loyalty

Boys- Are Loyal As A Good Dog Is To His Master.

Men- Are Loyal As A Good Master Is To His Dog.

I've seen a lot of people follow their boys into the flames in the name of loyalty. Boys will lose everything they have because their friend chose to. Men are loyal to the ones they love but have clear lines that they don't let people cross. Allowing people to control your decisions or bring you down with them because they know you're "loyal" isn't loyalty, it's being taken advantage of. Dogs are known for their loyalty; they will follow their master's commands no matter what the outcome might be. But unless you're okay with being the submissive one in your relationships, you have to be as loyal as the master is to his dog. The master is in control of his life and has his dog's back as well, but if that dog bites his hand enough, or pees on the carpet too much, the master has to decide when his loyalty to a disloyal dog ends.

BOYS

☐ Agree ☐ Disagree ☐ Both

VS

Why I feel this way

_____

_____

MEN

_____

_____

_____

_____

THE DEFINITION OF A MAN

_____

_____

My definition of _____

_____

_____

4- Courage

Boys- Are Afraid Of Rejection And Damaging Their Pride, So They Make Excuses Instead Of Attempts.

Men- May Be Afraid Of Rejection But Are More Concerned About Missing An Opportunity.

You going for that class? That girl? You taking that trip? You writing that song? And if you do, are you going to perform it? We all have reasons why we can't or shouldn't take the opportunities life puts in front of us. Boys attempt to be fearless but are run by fear. Boys operate out of fear, but as long as it looks like they have the power they're fine. You can control whether you try or not, and because of that, it feels like power. When I was younger there were always those girls that me and my boys would talk about. The ones we all wanted to talk to, but sometimes when the opportunity came, "Nah man I'm trying to get at this other girl" or, "No I said she's cool but I'm not trying to go over there right now." Cowards! All of us! I'm not saying we should have all tried to talk to every woman we thought was attractive, but had we not been so afraid of rejection (no, not just from the girls, but from our boys seeing us get shot down) we may have made a move. And the bigger the opportunity, the more fear boys feel, and the more excuses they make. I wanted to play basketball my freshman year and I went to tryouts... And I watched! I was dressed and prepared to play, but I just watched. It was fear. What if I played like trash? What if I didn't make it? Boys would rather take out the risk of rejection from the equation than to allow the opportunity for success. Boys live with much more regret than men because of this.

☐ Agree   ☐ Disagree   ☐ Both

BOYS VS MEN

Why I feel this way

_____

_____

_____

_____

_____

_____

_____

THE DEFINITION OF A MAN

_____

_____

My definition of _____

_____

_____

<u>Boys VS Men</u>
5- Anger

Boys- Get Angry And Make Decisions That Make The Situation Worse.

Men- Get Angry And Make Decisions To Improve Their Situation.

I've been saying this for years, "Anger isn't a bad thing!" There are no emotions that are "bad," it's how you feel. It's just how we express our anger that gets us into trouble. Nobody would say being happy is a bad thing, but if you express that happiness in a negative way, then it can be. If what you do when you're happy is hop in the car, hit the freeway and go 120 miles an hour, then your emotion is being expressed in a way that may lead to negative outcomes. Same as anger. Boys get mad and do things that just make everything worse for them. Men get angry and use that as motivation to change the situation. You mad? Do something about it then! Only a boy would get mad and bang their head on the wall like it's going to help them or hurt someone else.

BOYS
VS
MEN

☐ Agree   ☐ Disagree   ☐ Both

Why I feel this way

_____

_____

_____

_____

_____

_____

THE DEFINITION OF A MAN

_____

_____

My definition of _____

_____

_____

Boys VS Men
6- Progression

Boys- Measure Themselves In Comparison To Where Others Are In Life.

Men- Measure Themselves Based On Personal Progression.

We all start off somewhere in life, and it's not the same spot as everyone else. Where you were at last year VS where you're at today is a much more accurate measurement of progress than where you're at today VS where someone else is at. (Physically, Mentally, Spiritually Etc.) When I started writing music, if I would have compared myself to Tupac on day 1 I would have quit! Even though some people get lucky or are naturally gifted in one area of life, most of the time, it's not going to happen to you. Progress takes work. 12 years later, when I listen to my first songs, my progression is evident. You can hit the gym one time, see the guy benching 400 pounds and get in line next if you want to. But if you haven't put in that work to build up to it, and are trying to compare yourself to the person who did, you're always going to feel like you're not good enough.

BOYS

VS

MEN

THE DEFINITION OF A MAN

☐ Agree ☐ Disagree ☐ Both

Why I feel this way

_____

_____

_____

_____

_____

_____

_____

_____

_____

My definition of _____

_____

_____

Boys VS Men
7- Listening

Boys- Know When To Talk.

Men- Know When To Listen.

When I was younger I always had something to say. If I didn't like what you said or what you did, I was going to let you know. I always had an opinion I needed people to hear. I wasn't hearing anything other people were saying because I was always thinking about what I was going to say next. Sometimes the strongest voice needs to be the quietest. I remember a few times hearing someone talk disrespectful to an older guy, and he just stood there listening, didn't say a word. I asked him too, "Are you just going to let him talk to you like that?" (because you know, I always had something to say) and he just looked at me and said, "You weren't listening to a word he said were you?" It took me years to figure it out. You can't always let people know that you know the cards they're holding, because once you do, they change the way they play the game. Always having something to say isn't strength. Strength comes from knowing when to close your mouth and really listen.

☐ Agree ☐ Disagree ☐ Both

Why I feel this way

_____

_____

_____

_____

_____

_____

_____

_____

THE DEFINITION OF A MAN

_____

_____

My definition of _____

_____

_____

Boys VS Men

8- Perspective

Boys- Attempt To Solve The Same Problems Using The Same Failed Methods.

Men- Change The Equation.

If you play a sport, let's say basketball, and you're right handed with a defender guarding you who guards your right every time, you're not scoring unless you learn to go left. Simple as that! Boys would say, "I can only go right, so I'm going to keep going right and hope for the best." Men would look at the situation, see that what they're doing isn't working and try something new. If you keep getting in trouble for doing the same thing, stop trying to find a way to get away with it and find a way to get away <u>from it</u>. 1+1 will always equal 2! If you want a different outcome then the equation has to change.

BOYS
VS
MEN

☐ Agree ☐ Disagree ☐ Both

Why I feel this way

_____

_____

_____

_____

_____

_____

THE DEFINITION OF A MAN

_____

_____

My definition of _____

_____

_____

<u>Boys VS Men</u>
9- Revenge

Boys- Seek Revenge By Hurting Someone Else.

Men- Seek Revenge By Helping Themselves.

When someone hurts you, it is natural to feel the urge to hurt them back. I think for a boy or a man, this instinct is intact. However, men find opportunities to allow their success to be their strongest weapon against their enemies. Boys will use their energy to attempt to destroy their opponent, rather than to build themselves. If an adversary brings you down, and you focus on bringing them down in return, you might succeed, but bringing them down doesn't uplift you. Being on the same level doesn't bring you up to the level you're trying to reach. Boys will spend all day fighting each other in the flames, men try to find ways to escape the hell they're in.

☐ Agree   ☐ Disagree   ☐ Both

BOYS

VS

MEN

THE DEFINITION OF A MAN

Why I feel this way

_____

_____

_____

_____

_____

_____

_____

_____

My definition of _____

_____

_____

10- Instincts

Boys- Use Instincts As A Crutch To Not Grow.

Men- Create New Instincts That Revolve Around Progress.

I used to justify my decisions by saying things like, "That's just who I am," which was true but didn't mean I had to keep being who I was, or that I was incapable of changing my instincts. My instinct when being called certain names or being challenged to a fight was always to react with violence and sort it out later. Those instincts created far more trouble for me than was necessary. Some instincts are needed, and we can't deny the protection they provide. You would be foolish to deny instincts that life has taught you were needed for survival. But If we're talking about progress and growth, then reacting the same to the same situations will carry the same results. Boys stay on that hamster wheel going in circles because that's what they know. Men question the cage they're in and see the hamster as a fool for following the instincts that get them nowhere.

☐
Agree

☐
Disagree

☐
Both

Why I feel this way

BOYS
VS
MEN

THE DEFINITION OF A MAN

_____

_____

_____

_____

_____

_____

_____

_____

_____

My definition of _____

_____

_____

Boys VS Men
11- Problem Solving

Boys- Focus On The Who, Or The What Is To Blame When They're Upset.

Men- Focus On The "Why."

I'm not happy, who do I get mad at for it today? Anger used to be my best friend, we were boys! I never went anywhere without it. But as I got older, it wasn't enough to know I was mad and see who I could blame it on. I needed to know <u>WHY</u> I was upset. Sometimes I wasn't upset at all, but feeling a different emotion that I had been taught I wasn't allowed to feel, so mentally I just converted that emotion to anger. Sad? Disappointed? Underappreciated? Nope, just angry! When I started realizing the reasons I was mad, I could do something about it. You can get rid of all the people in your life that upset you, but until you figure out why they upset you, you'll have to get rid of anyone you ever meet, because they will all be blamed.

☐ Agree ☐ Disagree ☐ Both

BOYS

VS

MEN

Why I feel this way

_____

_____

_____

_____

_____

_____

_____

THE DEFINITION OF A MAN

_____

_____

My definition of _____

_____

_____

Boys VS Men
12- Friends

Boys- Surround Themselves With People That Agree With Them.

Men- Surround Themselves With People That Challenge Them.

Boys love their yes men! You know, the ones that laugh at their corny jokes like it's the funniest thing they've ever heard! Boys take it as a hit to their pride when they get challenged. I had a supervisor once that couldn't handle anyone disagreeing with him. Whenever I would suggest a different idea or point out a flaw in his plans, he would throw a fit like a toddler not being allowed to put his finger in a light socket. I have also been very fortunate to have worked with people in higher positions than me, that welcomed other people's input. Boys want to be right, they want credit and they want to be agreed with. Men want good outcomes even when it's a challenge to get them.

☐ Agree   ☐ Disagree   ☐ Both

Why I feel this way

BOYS

VS

MEN

THE DEFINITION OF A MAN

_____

_____

_____

_____

_____

_____

_____

_____

_____

My definition of _____

_____

_____

Boys VS Men
13- Advancing

Boys- Choose Not To Progress In Life So They Don't Leave Their Friends Behind.

Men- Always Move Forward And Extend The Invitation For Their Friends To Join Them.

Imagine a kid in 8th grade is about to graduate and he is told that his best friend has to re-do his 8th grade year because he didn't make grades. What's the boy who's graduating going to do? Is he going to stay back with his friend because they've been boys since kindergarten and he isn't going to leave him behind? No! He's going to high school next year! In a boy's mind he isn't going anywhere without his friend. Even if that's exactly where that will lead him, nowhere. Men will progress in their life with or without their loved ones. Because to stay where you are at, to stay around the ones you're comfortable with is to accept a fate created by others. Men will take a step and extend their hand to their friends to join them. But whether they are moving forward as a group, or alone, their feet don't stop moving.

BOYS

VS

MEN

Why I feel this way

_____

_____

_____

_____

_____

_____

THE DEFINITION OF A MAN

_____

_____

My definition of _____

_____

_____

Boys VS Men
14- Expectations

Boys- Set Goals Based On Expectations Set By Others.

Men- Set Goals Based On Ambition.

Most everyone has goals, but those who are in control of their own lives have goals based on what they want, not what other people want, or expect of them. When I was younger I had established myself a reputation, and even though it wasn't one that benefited me, I followed it, because it was who I was expected to be. I was expected to be crazy, loud, short-tempered, disrespectful to women, and overall not care what people thought, which was ironic because I acted that way to keep my reputation. When I grew up and had some time away from the people who expected me to be that way, I got a chance to consider my own goals and who I wanted to be. Men set goals based off ambition and allow that to fuel them to move forward instead of allowing others' expectations to keep them where they're at, or move in a direction they don't want to go.

☐ Agree ☐ Disagree ☐ Both

BOYS

VS

MEN

Why I feel this way

_____

_____

_____

_____

_____

_____

_____

THE DEFINITION OF A MAN

_____

_____

My definition of _____

_____

_____

Boys VS Men
15- Attitude

Boys- Make Plans And Expect Life To Adjust.

Men- Plan For Life Not To Go According To Their Plans.

Growing up I was a control FREAK! Life had to go how I told it to go or there was a problem. So it goes without saying that when I made plans, there was almost always a problem. Boys make plans and if things change they throw the whole thing away. Life won't always go the way you plan, men know this and find ways to make the best out of whatever happens. I grew up in California and had recently moved to Washington. I've been making music for over ten years and Seattle is a great place for music. I came to California to visit for Christmas, a bunch of family drama happened and I ended up staying there for 2 and a half years. That entire time I was there was against my plans. I could have done nothing during that time and complained, but I decided to take the opportunities that were there and find ways to make it positive for me, despite it not being my plan. During that time, I gained valuable work experiences, got the opportunity to be there for my family, get my credit right to buy a house when I moved back, saved money and I met my future wife. We don't have control over what life does, but our attitude about it is up to us.

BOYS

☐ Agree ☐ Disagree ☐ Both

VS

MEN

Why I feel this way

_____

_____

_____

_____

_____

_____

THE DEFINITION OF A MAN

_____

_____

My definition of _____

_____

_____

16- Hindsight

Boys- Attempt To Justify Their Decisions By Seeking Validation.

Men- Justify Their Decisions Based On Their Outcomes.

If it worked and you got the outcome you wanted, you need no validation. It's when things go wrong that boys start looking for yes men. When a boy makes a mistake, he looks around for anyone to agree with the decisions he has made so he feels justified in making them. Hindsight isn't to be trusted. Just because in the end you see that you would have ended up better off had you chose differently, it doesn't mean you made the wrong decision. You can go all in and win regardless of the cards you're holding, but taking that risk holding a bad hand is still not a smart decision. Men use hindsight, not to regret their decisions, but to grow from them.

□ Agree □ Disagree □ Both

BOYS
VS
MEN

Why I feel this way

_____

_____

_____

_____

_____

_____

_____

THE DEFINITION OF A MAN

_____

_____

My definition of _____

_____

_____

17- Capabilities

Boys- Say "I Don't Know How, I've Never Done It, So I Can't."

Men- Realize That Without A First Time Doing Something There Will Never Be A Second.

There was a time that everything was your first time doing it. Before we all took our first step we didn't know what we were doing, we just went for it, failed a bunch and learned it. Lack of knowledge in something is not the same as lack of ability. I'm sure we are all capable of success, but what if your success lies in a field or a talent you've never put any effort into? To deny success before you've even attempted is to embrace failure.

☐ Agree ☐ Disagree ☐ Both

Why I feel this way

BOYS
VS
MEN

THE DEFINITION OF A MAN

_____

_____

_____

_____

_____

_____

_____

_____

_____

My definition of _____

_____

_____

Boys VS Men
18- Self-Worth

Boys- Say What They Feel Needs To Be Said To Help Them In Their Current Situation.

Men- Say What They Believe And Stand Behind It No Matter The Situation.

Coming up, I talked to most people like they were cops and I was trying to stay out of jail. I just said whatever I needed to say, to get the best results from my current situation. That's such a cowardly way to live though. There are times in life where I understand why people felt they needed to lie. But for the most part, if you're man enough to do it, be man enough to own it. I've burnt a lot of bridges, I've lost friends, and the respect of others because I say and I do what I believe is right. But I stopped counting the losses because I haven't lost what's most important to me. I haven't lost my self-respect, morals, or vision. You don't have to like me, agree with me or want to be around me. And I don't have to care.

☐ Agree ☐ Disagree ☐ Both

BOYS

VS

MEN

THE DEFINITION OF A MAN

Why I feel this way

_____

_____

_____

_____

_____

_____

_____

_____

_____

My definition of _____

_____

_____

19- Integrity

Boys- Behavior Is Dictated By What Others Will Think About Them.

Men- Have Integrity And Allow That To Dictate Their Behavior.

I remember realizing this a little bit in middle school, and really having it sink in when I got into high school. Seeing my "friends" change how they acted depending on who was around. Trying to show off to make themselves look better or even talking and walking different depending on the situation. I saw some guys acting like they were auditioning for a movie role and I remember wondering who was real. As I got older I really understood the meaning of integrity. I was able to see the older guys navigate every situation they were in without changing masks. Not to say they weren't Bi-Social, but they stood by their morals and beliefs in every situation.

☐ Agree ☐ Disagree ☐ Both

BOYS

VS

MEN

Why I feel this way

_____

_____

_____

_____

_____

_____

_____

THE DEFINITION OF A MAN

_____

_____

My definition of _____

_____

_____

<u>Boys VS Men</u>
20- Work Ethic

Boys- Look For The Easy Way.

Men- Look For The Right Way.

Just because it sounds good doesn't mean it is good. Just because you feel like doing it, doesn't mean you should. And the easy way is rarely the right way something should be done. Not doing things the right way from the beginning usually makes more work for you later. When I was younger, especially when it was something I didn't want to do, I just wanted to get it over with. I remember one time me and my older brother were doing the dishes, I was probably around 8 years old and he was 10. We got done with the plates and silverware and what not, and we got down to the pots and pans, must have been 3 or 4 of them. Now this was mid-1990's, and we didn't have money for those Teflon or non-stick pans. We were scrubbing away for a little while and weren't making any progress. So my brother suggested hiding the pans and moving on with our day. It worked, but about a week later when my mom was outside planting flowers and found her pots and pans buried in the dirt, we not only had those dishes to do, but we were doing extra chores with a sore backside.

BOYS

VS

MEN

THE DEFINITION OF A MAN

☐ Agree ☐ Disagree ☐ Both

Why I feel this way

_____

_____

_____

_____

_____

_____

_____

_____

_____

_____

My definition of _____

_____

_____

Boys VS Men
21- Pride

Boys- Make Decisions They Know Will Hurt Them To Protect Their Pride.

Men- Know How To Stay Out Of Their Own Way.

Call it shooting yourself in the foot, tripping over your own shadow or getting in your own way; boys are masters of self-sabotage. It's part of that, "living in the moment" mentality that has gotten so misinterpreted. Boys act in the moment, like the next moment they don't have to live with the outcome of the previous moment. Nobody wants to be made to look a fool, whether it's by a teacher, coach, boss, random dude in the street, whatever. But as men, we should realize that nobody can make us look a fool more than ourselves. Pride can be a hard pill to swallow. But knowing that ultimately, no matter who said or did what, the way you responded is the reason you're in trouble; that's a bitter, much bigger pill to try and take.

☐ Agree ☐ Disagree ☐ Both

BOYS

VS

MEN

Why I feel this way

_____

_____

_____

_____

_____

_____

_____

THE DEFINITION OF A MAN

_____

_____

My definition of _____

_____

_____

22- Rightfulness

Boys- Expect Things Given First, And Deserved Later.

Men- Expect Nothing Undeserved.

You live long enough and you'll learn that there's no better teacher than life. When you're younger, your basic needs are usually met, that's the way it's supposed to work anyway. You get your food and shelter free. But when you get older, you can't barely breathe without paying taxes for the air you get. You earn it or you don't get it (men also understand sometimes you don't get it even after earning it) and when you think life owes you something, you're about to get taught one of life's greatest lessons. Nothing is for free. You don't always pay with money, but you're paying for it, and you're paying BEFORE you get it. Go ahead and pop into McDonald's and try to get that double cheeseburger before you get that $1 out ($1.08 after tax, because you're also paying for the right to pay for it) it won't happen. Boys think, "I'll get it because I deserve it" while men think, "I got it because I deserved it." It's after the fact. You don't get a check until after you put in the work.

☐ Agree ☐ Disagree ☐ Both

BOYS VS MEN

Why I feel this way

_____

_____

_____

_____

_____

_____

_____

_____

_____

THE DEFINITION OF A MAN

_____

_____

My definition of _____

_____

_____

<u>Boys VS Men</u>
23- Apologizing

Boys- Apologize With Words Or Gifts.

Men- Apologize By Changing Their Behavior.

When a 3-year-old kid hits their brother or sister, their mom will tell them to say sorry. A little while later, they hit them again and they say sorry, the next day they're back to hitting. Why? Because they don't understand it's wrong, so they don't mean it when they say sorry, and their actions don't change. They're just saying what they're told to say, or what they need to say. To apologize and not mean it means nothing. If a boy cheats on his girl and says, "sorry, I made a mistake, here go some flowers," but he keeps on cheating on her, how sorry is he? Men make mistakes too, but if they're really sorry for something, they don't continue to do it. Same as the young men that apologize while their laughing, you just look foolish and now your word means nothing.

BOYS

☐ Agree ☐ Disagree ☐ Both

Why I feel this way

_____

_____

_____

_____

_____

_____

_____

_____

_____

VS

MEN

THE DEFINITION OF A MAN

My definition of _____

_____

_____

Boys VS Men
24- Goals

Boys- Set Goals That Prioritize Their Wants.

Men- Hold Off On Wants Until They've Secured Their Needs.

I know people in their 20's and 30's who always look like their bank account is about to bust from being so full (Name brand everything, car looking like it should be in a music video, etc.) but they don't own their own home and they're living bad. Boys will own 20 pairs of shoes and not have a job. They'll have a $400 car payment and not have their own place to live. Boys will spend their money on things that make them look like they have money instead of investing it in themselves to actually have some one day. Men pay no attention to what they want until they have what they need. Doing the opposite is like buying the icing and you don't even have a cake to put it on.

☐ Agree   ☐ Disagree   ☐ Both

BOYS
VS
MEN

Why I feel this way

_____

_____

_____

_____

_____

THE DEFINITION OF A MAN

_____

_____

My definition of _____

_____

_____

25- Motivation

Boys- Fight Against Things.

Men- Fight For Things.

I have always loved fighting. It landed me in a lot of trouble, and in anger management as a boy. The boy in me wanted to fight against everything! I hated and still hate being told what to do, it's a battle I'm constantly engaged in. But now I don't fight against what I'm told to do, I fight for ways to do what I want. As a man, I fight for what I want and believe in; I fight for people instead of against the opposition. Things made a lot more sense for me when I stopped fighting just to fight, and I stopped fighting primarily against things and started fighting for things. There are always going to be more things in life that you don't want than you do want. You can fight against everything you don't like your entire life and still never get what you want, or you can focus your energy fighting for what it is you do want and get it.

☐ Agree ☐ Disagree ☐ Both

Why I feel this way

_____

_____

_____

_____

_____

_____

_____

_____

_____

_____

My definition of _____

_____

_____

<u>Boys VS Men</u>
26- Power

Boys- When They Gain Power They're Feared For Their Muscle.

Men- When They Gain Power They're Respected For Their Mind.

I used to look up to the guys with power because they were feared. Everyone bowed down to them and I wanted the same recognition from those around me. But it's a thin line between fear and respect. Those same guys who were feared, were also hated. They were talked bad about, lied to, and disrespected when they weren't around. Nobody was loyal to them, because they weren't loyal to anyone. As I got older I started having different heroes and I realized that I respected them, and had no fear of them. Admiration and respect are mirror images of fear. They may look the same, but they're actually exact opposites.

☐ Agree   ☐ Disagree   ☐ Both

BOYS
VS
MEN

Why I feel this way

_____

_____

_____

_____

_____

_____

THE DEFINITION OF A MAN

_____

_____

My definition of _____

_____

_____

<u>Boys VS Men</u>
27- Experience

Boys- Think They Know Because They Heard About It.

Men- Know They Don't Know Until They've Experienced It.

I am thankful for the many adverse experiences I endured throughout my life. There is no way I would be able to view the world from my perspective without them. I could have heard about these things, or read a book about them, but without living through them, my understanding would be very limited. I grew up in an extremely racist community where I couldn't be friends with people simply because I looked different. I have been pulled over more than 40 times and been in countless fights to defend my right to exist being the color I am. I could go on with examples, but my point is that there are a lot of places in America where this isn't the case. Which is a great thing, but without experiencing it, a lot of people can't understand it. Plus, it seems people who don't have to understand rarely will. Think of it like school vs. experience. You might have read about it, or studied it, but it's not the same without experiencing it. Boys attempt to undermine things they don't understand; men attempt to empathize with them.

☐ Agree ☐ Disagree ☐ Both

Why I feel this way

BOYS
VS
MEN

THE DEFINITION OF A MAN

_____
_____
_____
_____
_____
_____
_____
_____
_____
_____

My definition of _____

_____
_____

<u>Boys VS Men</u>
28- Moving Forward

Boys- Waste Time Complaining About Their Situation.

Men- Understand That Time Spent Complaining Is More Time Suffering.

We all need to vent. I vent about everything in life that gets me upset. From personal issues to social or political issues. You have to get that off your chest. But there's a line we should never cross if we intend to be successful through the issues. If you are speaking on it and moving past it, then cool. The problem comes when we complain and have no answer. Or when we complain in non-specific ways, "I hate my life," okay, "What do you hate about it?" "Everything!" ... If you can't be specific and pinpoint the things you don't like, you won't be able to change them. Boys complain and have no solution. A boy would complain about hating where he lives, or his friends, or his financial state but has no intention to change any of it. That's doing nothing but wasting the energy you could be putting towards changing something. Men vent, explore their options and make moves. Boys swim in their suffering instead of looking for a way out of the water.

☐ Agree   ☐ Disagree   ☐ Both

BOYS

VS

MEN

Why I feel this way

_____

_____

_____

_____

_____

_____

THE DEFINITION OF A MAN

_____

_____

My definition of _____

_____

_____

29- Ambition

Boys- Look For The Finish Line.

Men- Look For The Next Race.

When you wait for something to end before you begin the next thing you already started late. It's like reading a book, when you get to the end of the page, if you don't turn to the next before you're done with the one you're on, there'll be a pause. If you want to be able to move ahead, you have to limit these pauses. Men think multiple steps ahead. When one thing is coming to an end, they look for where to start the next. Boys just want to be done with what they're doing, men understand that the end of one thing is just the beginning of another.

☐ Agree   ☐ Disagree   ☐ Both

Why I feel this way

_____

_____

_____

_____

_____

_____

_____

_____

_____

_____

My definition of _____

_____

_____

<u>Boys VS Men</u>
30- Priorities

Boys- Will Bet What They Hold Most Important To Gain Things They Can Live Without.

Men- Never Bet Anything They're Not Willing To Lose.

If I told you I'd bet you my $10 VS your car you wouldn't take that bet because you're risking way more than you have an opportunity to gain. Boys will make decisions that risk what they care most about (their life, freedom, future, girlfriend, etc.) for things they can live without (a little money, pride, cute girl, etc.). Men take risks too, but they're calculated risks. If the reward is worth the risk they consider taking the chance, but if any of their top priorities could be risked in the process, they won't do it at all.

BOYS

VS

MEN

THE DEFINITION OF A MAN

☐ Agree ☐ Disagree ☐ Both

Why I feel this way

_____

_____

_____

_____

_____

_____

_____

_____

_____

My definition of _____

_____

_____

<u>Boys VS Men</u>
31- Effort

Boys- Give The Amount Of Effort To Something They Think It Should Take.

Men- Give All The Effort They Have.

I remember playing sports as a kid and every once in a while, we would play against a team we knew we were better than, easy wins. But sometimes those games were the hardest to win because my team barely tried. We didn't stick to the game plan, did things we would have never done if we were playing against harder competition and made easy wins stressful by keeping the game close until the end. Boys relax and try the minimum they think they should have to try to get the results they want. As I got older, I realized that trying to put forth less effort made me have to work so much harder in the long run.

BOYS

☐ Agree   ☐ Disagree   ☐ Both

Why I feel this way

_____

_____

VS

_____

_____

MEN

_____

_____

_____

THE DEFINITION OF A MAN

_____

_____

My definition of _____

_____

_____

32- Time

Boys- Continuously Invest In A Mistake So They Don't Have To Admit It.

Men- Stop Investing Their Time And Energy When They Get Nothing In Return.

That dirt on your hands won't ever completely go away by wiping it on your shirt, you're just spreading it around and making things worse. You have to wash your hands to get rid of it. I couldn't tell you how many ideas, things, and people I have had to stop investing in. Not just talking about financially, and no, time isn't money, it's far more valuable. You can check your bank account and see how much money you have, but none of us know how much time we have left. We can't afford to waste our time on mistakes. Men admit their mistakes, look for a way to ensure they don't waste more time making the same mistake in the future, and wash their hands.

☐   ☐   ☐

Agree   Disagree   Both

BOYS

VS

MEN

Why I feel this way

_____

_____

_____

_____

_____

THE DEFINITION OF A MAN

_____

_____

My definition of _____

_____

_____

33- Determination

Boys- Chase What They Want.

Men- Find Ways To Make What They Want Stop Running.

Chasing money, women, progress, material things? At some point, we need to ask ourselves what we're doing that makes the things we want run away from us. Boys chase things without having a net to catch what they want even if they got close enough to reach it. Men stop running, sit down and figure out how to make what they want in life come to them. If you're moving without knowing the steps you need to take to get where you want to be, how can you reach your destination?

☐ Agree   ☐ Disagree   ☐ Both

Why I feel this way

_____

_____

_____

_____

_____

_____

_____

_____

BOYS

VS

MEN

THE DEFINITION OF A MAN

My definition of _____

_____

_____

34- Opinions

Boys- Have strong opinions Based Off Other People's.

Men- Have Strong Opinions Based Off Their Own Beliefs.

I used to work with this middle school student who would always say how much he hated Obama. I typically don't get involved in political discussions with children, but after about 6 months of hearing it, I finally asked, "Why do you hate Obama so much?" he replied, "He's just awful, he's a bad president." I asked, "Why?" and he had no idea why he hated him so much. He just did! Because that's what he heard. Men have reasons they feel the way they do. Whether I agree or disagree with a man's beliefs, it's a whole lot easier to respect them when they know why they feel the way they do.

□ Agree   □ Disagree   □ Both

BOYS

VS

MEN

Why I feel this way

_____

_____

_____

_____

_____

_____

THE DEFINITION OF A MAN

_____

_____

My definition of _____

_____

_____

35- Strength

Boys- Feel Strength While They Slowly Pour Salt On The Snail And Watch It Die.

Men- Feel Strength When They Move The Snail Out Of The Walkway To Ensure It Doesn't Get Stepped On.

I've been around so many people in my life that just want to destroy things, people, ideas, etc. But anyone, any age can destroy something, it's not a special skill or quality to break things. To recognize the strength you have and not take advantage of it is the real power. Yes, you can destroy that which is weaker than you, but can you protect it? Men feel strength by building something and watching it grow, boys feel strength by enforcing their will on that which is weaker. To have power means nothing, to have control over the power you have is the real strength.

☐ Agree ☐ Disagree ☐ Both

Why I feel this way

BOYS
VS
MEN

THE DEFINITION OF A MAN

_____

_____

_____

_____

_____

_____

_____

_____

My definition of _____

_____

_____

36- Confidence

Boys- Express Cockiness.

Men- Express Confidence.

I am an extremely confident person. I know what I'm good at, and I know I am capable of doing anything in this world. I've been called cocky on more occasions than I can remember and at times found it hard to explain what I feel the difference is. I think boys express their confidence as cockiness because they need to feel better than someone else due to their talent or skill. They need a reason to hold their head high. While men use their abilities to inspire others. It all comes down to intent. Cockiness is, "Look what I can do, I'm better than you," and confidence is knowing you can do something well and not having to brag about it. I have never met a cocky man that didn't come off looking like a boy. Confidence means to know, cockiness means to be unsure and need validation.

BOYS VS MEN

THE DEFINITION OF A MAN

☐ Agree   ☐ Disagree   ☐ Both

Why I feel this way

_____

_____

_____

_____

_____

_____

_____

_____

_____

_____

My definition of _____

_____

_____

37- Conflict

Boys- Refuse To Participate When Forced To Work With An Adversary.

Men- Focus On The Task And Not The Partner.

I've never been one to bite my tongue and pretend to be someone or something I'm not. As a boy that meant telling you exactly how I feel about you and if I didn't like you, you knew it. I wasn't working with you, talking to you or even acknowledging you. I've had supervisors and co-workers I couldn't stand, just personalities didn't mix. But the older you get, the more you'll realize there are more people you'll disagree with than you'll agree with. Which is a good thing I guess because I like my circle small. But there will be times that you must choose to either ignore your differences, or fail. You either do the project or you fail, you go to work and get along with that person you can't stand or you're fired. I don't know about you, I'll lose things for those I love, but I'm not losing things for people I don't even like. Boys allow the fact that they don't like someone to hurt them. Men focus on what needs to be done and find ways to get it done despite the people involved. If they understand this they'll do the same, if not, allow the boy in them to back out and you won't have to worry about it.

☐ Agree ☐ Disagree ☐ Both

Why I feel this way

_____

_____

_____

_____

_____

_____

_____

_____

_____

My definition of _____

_____

_____

38- Competition

Boys- Rarely Enter Into Competitions They Feel They Won't Win.

Men- Look Competition In The Face And Smile At The Opportunity To Beat It.

I've never met a single person that enjoys losing. Some people take it harder than others based on how competitive they are, but never have I seen someone feel joy in losing. Boys will see the competition, see that the odds aren't in their favor and choose not to compete. Because it doesn't feel good to lose. But a man's motivation isn't how bad it feels to lose; it's how great it feels to win. Whether it's a new job opportunity you don't think you have the experience to handle, a school you don't feel you're smart enough to get into, or a sports team. You won't always win at everything, but you'll never win if you don't try.

☐ Agree   ☐ Disagree   ☐ Both

BOYS

Why I feel this way

_____

_____

VS

_____

_____

MEN

_____

_____

_____

THE DEFINITION OF A MAN

_____

_____

My definition of _____

_____

_____

39- Dedication

Boys- Hope To Be Lucky.

Men- Work To Be Deserving.

No matter how lucky you are, or are hoping to be, luck without work still leads to failure. A boy would beg to get a shot at something, spend his time trying to be lucky enough to get the chance, and then when the chance comes he isn't prepared to take advantage of it. I have a friend who has always worked to become the best basketball player he could be. In high school while we were all partying and hanging out late, he was home or in the gym. He got a free education and countless opportunities because of his commitment. It takes that type of dedication and sacrifice to become successful in anything you want to become. Boys wait for the opportunity; men prepare for it.

☐ Agree ☐ Disagree ☐ Both

BOYS VS MEN

THE DEFINITION OF A MAN

Why I feel this way

_____

_____

_____

_____

_____

_____

_____

_____

_____

My definition of _____

_____

_____

<u>Boys VS Men</u>
40- Forgiveness

Boys- See Forgiveness As A Way To Release Burden From The Other Person.

Men- See Forgiveness As A Way To Release The Burden From Themselves.

My father wasn't around when I was a boy. He somewhat tried to come back around every once in a while when I was in middle school but never was really there. I had a lot of anger towards him and before he died I hadn't spoken to him in years. I got a phone call saying he was in the hospital and I went to see him. He looked awful and for the first time I wasn't mad at him, I just felt bad for him. Doctors said he wasn't going to make it and for the next few weeks before he passed, I'd go to the hospital almost every day to see him. We didn't talk much though, he was either out of it and couldn't talk or I didn't have anything to say to him. I remember thinking, "I should say something to make him feel better, patch things up before he dies, but he doesn't deserve to be forgiven" then it hit me...I deserve to forgive him. I got stuff off my chest, told him how I felt and I forgave him. I'd like to think it meant something to him, but I honestly don't think it did. I'm just glad I let go of all the hatred and anger I had towards him before he left so it could go with him.

A boy would carry that weight their entire life so they don't have to forgive the person they're mad at or who hurt them. A man doesn't wait to be asked for forgiveness or for the forgiveness to be earned, he forgives. Not to release the other person, but to be free themselves.

☐ Agree   ☐ Disagree   ☐ Both

BOYS VS MEN

THE DEFINITION OF A MAN

Why I feel this way

_____

_____

_____

_____

_____

_____

_____

My definition of _____

_____

_____

<u>Boys VS Men</u>
41- Culture

Boys- Respect Other People Based On Their Own Personal Values.

Men- Respect Other People's Values.

Black and white, no grey. That's how the world is viewed through the eyes of boys. Life is not that simple. Views are created and instilled within us based on multiple variables. Background, history, beliefs and reinforced opinions. If you believe something, there's a reason, and if someone thinks the opposite or differently, there's a reason for that too. You don't have to agree, or even understand a person's views to respect them. Example: There are starving people in America that would never consider eating a cat or dog. There are countries that wouldn't think twice. There are also countries with starving people that are surrounded by cows and they never consider eating them. While in America, beef has always been the most eaten meat. If you were born or raised in someone else's shoes your feet would smell the same. Boys attempt to have truth other than their own, men understand that though there are some definite truths in this world, most depend on who you ask.

☐ Agree   ☐ Disagree   ☐ Both

BOYS
VS
MEN

THE DEFINITION OF A MAN

Why I feel this way

_____

_____

_____

_____

_____

_____

_____

_____

My definition of _____

_____

_____

42- Actions

Boys- Simply Talk About What They'll Do.

Men- Let Their Actions Do The Talking.

Boys love to tell stories about what they're going to do. They'll spend so much time talking about what they're going to do that they won't have any time or energy left to do it! All that talking might work for a while, but don't back it up one time and see what happens. I went from a boy running his mouth to a man of my word. I can't do it anymore. You could be a great basketball player and talk about how you're about to score 50 and win by 25. But if you get out there, score 42 and win by 20, you still didn't cash that check your mouth was writing. You the best basketball player? The best rapper? The best writer? Actor? Etc. Don't talk about it, any boy could do that. Be a man and prove it.

☐ Agree   ☐ Disagree   ☐ Both

BOYS
VS
MEN

Why I feel this way

_____

_____

_____

_____

_____

_____

THE DEFINITION OF A MAN

_____

_____

My definition of _____

_____

_____

43- Appreciation

Boys- Aren't Happy Until They Reach Their Destination.

Men- Find Happiness In The Steps They're Taking.

Personal growth is almost solely dependent on wanting better. Pushing yourself and the limits to get to where you want to be in life. But if you don't make the choice to appreciate what you have now, while you work on getting more, you'll lose what you have now. Then when you reach your goal, you won't appreciate that because you'll no longer have what you had before, and be miserable losing what you just got in a search for what you had. That's a tiring circle, but it's much more tiring running it than reading it. Boys are constantly unhappy because there's always something else they want. If your happiness is dependent on turning the page, then you'll never be happy. Because as soon as you turn the page, you see that the book continues on the next. It's a choice to be happy. I remember being younger and feeling like being happy in my current situation was the same as becoming complacent, so I chose not to be happy. It's not, it's just a man's decision to enjoy the road trip instead of complaining that the destination's too far away. As long as he's moving forward, a man appreciates the steps he's taking.

☐ Agree   ☐ Disagree   ☐ Both

BOYS

VS

MEN

THE DEFINITION OF A MAN

Why I feel this way

_____

_____

_____

_____

_____

_____

_____

_____

_____

My definition of _____

_____

_____

Boys VS Men
44- Independence

Boys- Survive By Living In A Constant State Of Dependency.

Men- Are In Control Of their Own Freedom.

Overall independence should be rooted in all aspects of your life. Independence means your actions, thoughts, motives and decisions are your own. Being independent doesn't mean that you don't need help from time to time. It means that even when you need some support, you still stand on your own two feet. It's to have control over your own life. Boys not only ask for help when they need it, they ask for help as often as possible and attempt to get as much as possible. When men need assistance, they ask for, accept, and only allow the bare minimum with repayment being a top priority. Boys take what they can get because they have no intention of paying it back. Men understand that though it's okay to get help when needed, they should see it as a loan and not a gift.

☐ Agree   ☐ Disagree   ☐ Both

BOYS

VS

MEN

THE DEFINITION OF A MAN

Why I feel this way

_____

_____

_____

_____

_____

_____

_____

_____

_____

My definition of _____

_____

_____

<u>Boys VS Men</u>
45- Respect

Boys- Wait To Give Respect Until Someone Earns It.

Men- Give Respect Until Someone Loses It.

My boys and I used to do our own thing and we didn't care what people thought or how it affected them. We started off making people have no respect for us because we started off showing we had none for them. And then when there was a confrontation or disagreement, we would demand respect we never deserved. Boys are afraid that people won't respect them, so they don't give people the opportunity to. Men give the opportunity to be respected, and show respect until someone proves they don't deserve it.

☐   ☐   ☐

Agree   Disagree   Both

Why I feel this way

_____

_____

_____

_____

_____

_____

_____

_____

_____

_____

My definition of _____

_____

_____

46- Leadership

Boys- Lead By Force.

Men- Lead By Example.

Boys get into positions of leadership, (captain of a team, supervisor, manager, position of office etc.) gain power over others and make them do things they never would. I've had supervisors who bark orders, talk to people like they're worthless and make them do things that they're "too good" to do themselves. If you're not willing to do it yourself and do it first, you shouldn't ask someone else to. It's also hard for someone to follow you if you aren't in the front. Being in a position of power and leadership means you do more work, not less. Boys try to lead from the protection of being in the back of the group. Men lead from the front, as the protection of the group.

BOYS VS MEN

THE DEFINITION OF A MAN

☐ Agree ☐ Disagree ☐ Both

Why I feel this way

_____

_____

_____

_____

_____

_____

_____

_____

_____

My definition of _____

_____

_____

47- Consistency

Boys- Change Their Opinions Based On Who's Present.

Men- Don't Apologize For Being True To Themselves.

No matter what you do, there will be people who hate you for it, that's a fact. You can pretend to be someone you think people will like, and those who may have actually liked who you are, will hate you for being who you're pretending to be. You can be the best and be hated for it, the worst, average or not even try. You can never satisfy or be liked by everyone. Allen Iverson was one of my favorite basketball players, and I don't think anyone in the league has ever been loved and hated as much as him. There wasn't really room in the middle with the strong personality he had. You either loved him for being true to himself, or you hated him for it. But what I always respected about him is that he was unapologetically him. Whether you loved him or hated him, at least you felt that way about who he truly was. Boys pretend to be, think, act and believe to be something they're not, based on who is around. Men are consistent. They don't apologize or make excuses for being themselves. They would rather be hated for who they are than loved for something they're not.

☐ Agree ☐ Disagree ☐ Both

BOYS

VS

MEN

Why I feel this way

_____

_____

_____

_____

_____

_____

THE DEFINITION OF A MAN

_____

_____

My definition of _____

_____

_____

48- Humility

Boys- Rank Their Importance In The World.

Men- Are Humbled By It.

Humility carries with it so many other characteristics that are impossible to have without it. If you're not humble, you can't truly be compassionate, loving, generous or caring because to be those things you have to have the ability to look outside yourself. You have to understand you're not better than someone to truly love them, or the love you have for yourself will always come first. You can't be compassionate towards someone else if you think you're more important or you'll constantly think about how it affects you and take the focus off of them. Boys see their ability, intellect and accomplishments as a reflection of their importance. Men see that we are all one and our importance is relative to what or who we effect. All life on Earth is dependent on the sun but the sun is just one of many stars, and the Earth seems big until you compare it to other planets. We should all strive for greatness, but never forget how small we truly are.

☐ Agree ☐ Disagree ☐ Both

BOYS

Why I feel this way

_____

_____

_____

_____

_____

_____

VS

MEN

_____

_____

THE DEFINITION OF A MAN

_____

_____

My definition of _____

_____

_____

49- Freedom

Boys- Are Confined By Their Bodies.

Men- Are Freed By Their Minds.

My mother will deny this until the end of time, but when I was a kid, my brother and I spent a lot of our summers outside, and not by choice. Don't get me wrong, we had a lot of great times and I'm happy for it, but it doesn't change the fact that it wasn't our choice. I know It couldn't have been easy raising 4 kids in a 2 bedroom, 500 square foot house, and my brother and I (mostly me) probably made that place feel a lot smaller being as active and loud as we were. We would get up real early, go to the living room and watch TV as quietly as we could so we didn't wake my mom up, because as soon as she was up we ate breakfast and were sent outside until dinner. We were never allowed to leave the yard and had to find ways to keep ourselves entertained. At this time, we were in a house with a very small front yard, tiny fence with grapes that grew on it, and one tree. This was Northern California where summers were 110 degrees plus sometimes. We had to find ways to keep ourselves entertained. We hit a ball we found with a piece of wood like it was baseball, (well, one time because after the first hit a piece of the stick broke off and went into my arm) we caught frogs, dug holes, climbed the tree, and figured out that if you hold two dragonflies together they fight until one is decapitated. Good times! Freedom is often an illusion, the amount you believe in it is as real as you allow it to become. We were confined to a small area and weren't allowed to leave, but no matter how confined our bodies were, our minds were always free. Boys are limited to their bodies' abilities, while men are as free as their mind is.

☐ Agree   ☐ Disagree   ☐ Both

BOYS VS MEN

Why I feel this way

_____

_____

_____

_____

_____

THE DEFINITION OF A MAN

_____

_____

My definition of _____

_____

_____

Boys VS Men
50- Accepting

Boys- Tolerate People Who Are Different.

Men- Accept Them.

I have always hated the term "tolerance." You hear it all the time, like tolerating someone or something is being positive towards it. I always hear people being told to be tolerant. It seems like we're missing the point. To tolerate is to put up with something even though if you had the choice you'd get rid of it, or change it. You tolerate a broken arm, a loud neighbor or the smell in your bathroom when you run out of spray. If you apply the feeling of tolerance toward how you treat or view people, those people become an unwanted or undesirable presence that exist around you that you would much rather get rid of. Being accepting toward someone means to see them for who they are, and even if you disagree with them, you accept them for being different than you are. Boys tolerate people because they have to, men make the choice to accept them.

☐ Agree   ☐ Disagree   ☐ Both

Why I feel this way

_____

_____

_____

_____

_____

_____

_____

_____

My definition of _____

_____

_____

<u>Boys VS Men</u>
51- Passion/Purpose

Boys- Search For Something To Live For.

Men- Search For Something Worth Dying For.

When you're younger people often ask you what you want to be when you "grow up." I always took that question as if there was going to be a time when you reach that goal and you're done, you've figured it all out. That's the furthest thing from the truth. We work to live and that's fine, I've come to terms with that. But I refuse to have my life revolve around work. I learned to flip that. Work revolves around my life. My work will be an extension of the passions I have. We all have to earn money, but what would you do, what would your purpose be if you didn't have to worry about money? Boys live their entire life finding new things to live for. Men see a picture bigger than themselves and let their passion in life, be worth dying for.

☐ Agree ☐ Disagree ☐ Both

Why I feel this way

BOYS

VS

MEN

THE DEFINITION OF A MAN

_____

_____

_____

_____

_____

_____

_____

_____

My definition of _____

_____

_____

Boys VS Men
52- Happiness

Boys- Look Outward To Find It In Material Things.

Men- Look Inside Themselves.

I grew up in a family without much money. I had to do without a lot
of material things I wanted. I spent some of my teen years making
quick money, and a lot of it. My early adult years I was broke,
working multiple jobs and I've had good paying jobs where money
wasn't an issue. The number one happiest memory I have is back
when I was around 9. My mother worked at the school so she was
home with us during the summer and we got to spend a lot of time
together. Almost every morning, my brother and I would pull out
this big plastic storage container that my mom kept under her bed
full of change. We would gather up some change and go to the
store with my mom. We got to pick out a snack while she got her
morning Pepsi. But the best part was that we would go back home,
and spend hours playing Monopoly. I don't know how she did it, but
even without that much money, I never felt poor. I am very lucky
because I never knew we didn't have money until I looked back on
things. We rarely remember the things we didn't have and the fact
that we didn't have them, but we will remember what we did have
and the feelings associated with them. Spoiled kids and adults are
some of the most miserable people. They're constantly unhappy
even though they have exactly what we think should make them
happy. Because they focus on getting more instead of putting the
focus on what they have. Boys add up their belongings to count
their happiness. Men count their blessings.

☐ Agree   ☐ Disagree   ☐ Both

Why I feel this way

_____

_____

_____

_____

_____

_____

_____

My definition of _____

_____

_____

Afterword

This is the start, it's not where it ends. We will continuously be told what it is to be a man. Until the end of our lives we will constantly be guided to blindly follow outside perspectives without developing our own. It's a choice. To either open our mouths and be force-fed other people's definitions of a man, or open our mouth to express our own. You will be held accountable for your actions, not the outside world or opinions that inspired them, so you should definitely be sure that the way you think, live and act are decisions you consciously made.

You only know what you know and the decisions you make daily are based off of that information. The 15-year-old me wouldn't make the same decisions the 25-year-old me would have made, and the 35-year-old me will make better decisions than I would today. Don't allow hindsight to make you feel inadequate. Allow it to inspire you.

"Unless you have lived this life once before, don't allow hindsight the power to create regret."

-1 Luv

"I've spent years working at youth centers, juvenile detention centers, group homes, schools, military institutions, and churches. I have built and facilitated hundreds of programs and the biggest progress I have ever seen in people has been through programs built in a way that allows open-minded conversations. Now I'm here, at a point in my life where everything seems to have intentionally brought me to."

Made in the USA
Middletown, DE
27 November 2018